National Parks

PUZZLE BOOK

USA GRAB A PENCIL PRESS

CARLISLE, MASSACHUSETTS

National Parks
PUZZLE BOOK

You are the part-owner of 84 million acres of the world's most treasured landscapes, ecosystems, and historical sites—all protected in America's more than 400 national parks. National parks teach us about cultural heritage, show us beautiful places, mark the grounds where important events took place, and commemorate national heroes. In a 1936 speech President Franklin D. Roosevelt declared: "There is nothing so American as our national parks.... The fundamental idea behind the parks...is that the country belongs to the people, that it is in process of making for the enrichment of the lives of all of us." Thanks to the National Park System, everyone has the opportunity to learn more about the history, culture, and natural landscapes that surround them, because national parks are everywhere:

STATUE OF LIBERTY NATIONAL MONUMENT

urban places, wild places, sacred and historic places. In this book you'll learn about the different kinds of places that are preserved and memorialized by the NPS.

It's hard to imagine, but over 300 million people visit a national park every year. That's a lot of people! NPS has hundreds of parks and memorials all over the country for everyone to visit. Some parks are famous for their natural beauty and awe-inspiring landscapes, like Rocky Mountain National Park, Grand Canyon National Park, and Yosemite National Park. Read on and you'll learn all about these amazing parks as well as the incredible natural diversity of America.

But that's not all. In this book you'll also learn about historical parks that preserve the nation's history and memorialize important historic figures, like presidents, leaders, and individuals who helped shape the country. You'll learn about the parks that preserve battlegrounds and memorialize the people who fought there, like Gettysburg National Military Park. You will also learn about cultural sites that preserve difficult and sad stories, like the Trail of Tears National Historic Trail and Manzanar National Historic Site. As you make your way through this puzzle book, you will learn that national parks preserve—in addition to nature—all types of history and culture in all types of places.

It's important to know, too, that the NPS does more than make parks (and their stories) available to its many visitors. It also plays an important role in protecting and managing natural resources. President John F. Kennedy said in a speech that "[i]t is the course of wisdom to set aside an ample portion of our natural resources as national parks and reserves, thus ensuring that future generations may know the majesty of the earth as we know it today." These words are just as true today as when Kennedy spoke them in 1962.

There is much to learn about the national parks, so get started on those puzzles!

PUZZLE ANSWERS ON BACK PAGES

America's Top Ten Most Visited National Parks

People love America's national parks. Over 300 million people visit a national park every year. Because America is such a large and geographically diverse country, its national parks are amazingly varied: They contain forests, deserts, rivers, waterfalls, glaciers, underwater reefs, mountains, islands, marshes, canyons, urban areas, and so much more. Each park is unique unto itself and its region. Unscramble the words below to discover America's ten most visited national parks.

RTEGA MSKOY MUSIANOTN = _____

GNADR NAYCNO = _____

OEYSIMET = _____

ELWYLONSOTE = _____

YOCKR NMIOAUTN = _____

CPIMYLO = _____

INOZ = _____

NGADR TNOTE = _____

CDAAIA = _____

CIGRELA = _____

Nature

```
H J Z C L E F R I V E R A V D P
W O R X L S E O S F J A D A I H
I F I Y I B E A R S N K M C B V
L E N K P F X A R E F P F A B P
D S X S C L A P E C S D H T K C
E S Y P A E Y C O A C T U I E A
R D B E L D B D S N A Y S O E M
N Y A U D O G W I Y J G P N A P
E C Q B P U R O P O B A D S G I
S I G H T S E E T N G D O N B N
S C T O U T S I D E S F I I O G
P C Q H A O S C P D L A T P V Z
H I K I N G T D C N T R E E S A
D M B F C P N S Y N X M K A L Y
G D A E D B E A U T Y E M A D A
E W I L D I C O S K A G I O R T
A T H S U P M S P R O T E C T P
```

Find the following:

RIVER
TREES
HIKING
VACATION
WILDERNESS
CANYON
BEARS
BEAUTY
EXPLORE
PROTECT
MOUNTAIN
CAMPING
OUTSIDE
SIGHTSEE
FOREST

MOOSE

GREAT SMOKY MOUNTAINS NATIONAL PARK
PHOTO: BILLY HATHORN

Great Smoky Mountains

ACROSS

2. This park is one of the largest protected areas in the eastern United States and comprises over 520 ___ acres.

4. The park is famous for its black ___ population.

5. The Great Smoky Mountains National Park is the ___ visited national park in all of America.

6. Fly ___ come to the park to fish the native trout that can be found in its waters.

8. In the 1800s the timber industry clear-cut old ___ from much of the region, before it was a park.

9. The park was originally homeland to the Cherokee, before westward expansion by Europeans pushed the American ___ out of the region.

10. Many of the trails in the park were created by the Civilian Conservation Corps, a federal program that created jobs during the ___ Depression.

11. Aside from sightseeing, the most popular activity in the park is ___.

DOWN

1. The Appalachian Trail stretches from Georgia all the way up to ___, and it passes through the center of the park.

2. The border between ___ and North Carolina runs through the center of the park.

3. John D. Rockefeller Jr. contributed 5 million ___ toward the creation of the park.

7. The Great Smoky ___ are part of the Appalachian Mountain chain.

Grand Canyon

ACROSS

2. The Grand Canyon became a ___ park in 1919.

5. John Wesley Powell led the ___ expedition by Europeans through the canyon in 1869.

7. The Colorado ___ runs through the canyon.

9. On average, the Grand Canyon is a ___ deep.

10. The Grand Canyon is a UNESCO World Heritage Site; UNESCO stands for ___ Nations Educational, Scientific, and Cultural Organization.

13. At its widest point, the canyon is 18 miles ___.

DOWN

1. The oldest ___ at the bottom of the canyon is close to 2 billion years old

3. The southwestern portion of the canyon is bordered by two ___ Indian reservations: the Havasupai Indian Reservation and the Hualapai Indian Reservation.

4. The visible ___ of rock in the canyon walls provide valuable geological information for scientists.

6. The Havasupai are an American Indian ___ that has called the Grand Canyon home for centuries.

8. Grand Canyon National Park is so popular that it has over 5 million ___ every year.

11. The steep canyon ___ were created by 5 million to 6 million years of erosion by the Colorado River.

12. This enormous canyon is located in the northwestern part of the state of ___.

National Park Service

The National Park Service (NPS) oversees and safeguards hundreds of places. But the NPS doesn't just take care of these special places; it makes them accessible to millions of visitors every year. The NPS also plays an important role in preserving local history and maintaining the heritage of communities that hold strong ties to these lands. Learn more about the NPS and its history with these two puzzles.

First, unscramble the words below, then use them to fill in the blanks in the next activity.

TAC =	_____
AINTNOLA AKSPR =	_____
CAER =	_____
ERNEGY =	_____
MLNIOIL =	_____
TSEAT =	_____
ISITVED =	_____
ELLYOWOESTN =	_____
HTWIE OSHUE =	_____
ROEAARWDH =	_____

Now use the unscrambled words to fill in the blanks below.

1. The NPS is a bureau of the U.S. Department of the Interior, which was established to manage and protect America's land, water, wildlife, and ___ resources.

2. The official emblem of the NPS is an ___ with a sequoia tree, bison, river, and mountain pictured inside.

3. President Woodrow Wilson signed the ___ that created the NPS in 1916.

4. The ___ ___ is part of the National Park System.

5. In addition to overseeing ___ ___, the NPS also oversees areas such as battlefields, monuments, military parks, historical parks, historic sites, lakeshores, seashores, recreation areas, scenic rivers, and trails.

6. The smallest national park site is Thaddeus Kosciuszko National Memorial, and it is only .02 ___.

7. Wrangell—St. Elias National Park and Preserve in Alaska is the largest national park site at 13.2 ___ acres.

8. ___ National Park was the nation's first national park, established in 1872.

9. The NPS oversees areas in every ___, as well the District of Columbia, American Samoa, Guam, Puerto Rico, and the Virgin Islands.

10. The Great Smoky Mountains National Park is the most ___ of all the national parks.

YELLOWSTONE NATIONAL PARK

Military Parks

ACROSS

2. Shiloh National Military Park in Tennessee and Mississippi is the site of one of the bloodiest Civil War battles. There were more ___ at Shiloh than in all of America's previous wars combined.

3. Fort Necessity National Battlefield in Pennsylvania preserves the 1754 ___ and Indian War battle site named after the fort.

5. Antietam National Battlefield in Sharpsburg, Maryland, is the site of the 1862 Civil War battle and includes the battlefield, a visitor ___, a national military cemetery, and multiple historic structures.

7. Technically not a ___ park, the Little Bighorn Battlefield National Monument in Montana preserves the site of the 1876 battle where General George Custer lost to the Lakota, Cheyenne, and Arapaho.

8. Gettysburg National Military Park in Pennsylvania preserves the site of the battle and tells the story of the Union victory that was a turning point for the ___ in the American Civil War.

9. In 1862 the Battle of Pea Ridge was fought to secure Missouri for the ___; it was a pivotal Civil War battle and is memorialized at the Pea Ridge National Military Park in Arkansas.

DOWN

1. Kings Mountain National Military Park is a ___ War park and is located in South Carolina, where most of the Revolutionary War battles and skirmishes occurred.

3. Chickamauga and Chattanooga National Military Park in Tennessee and Georgia was the ___ national military park and was established by Congress in 1890.

4. During the ___ War, Union and Confederate armies clashed many times on battlefields at Fredericksburg, Chancellorsville, Wilderness, and Spotsylvania. They are all protected as part of Fredericksburg & Spotsylvania National Military Park in Virginia.

6. Andrew Jackson and his men defeated Chief Menawa and his band of a thousand warriors in 1814, ending the Creek ___ at what is now Horseshoe Bend National Military Park in Alabama.

7. Vicksburg National Military Park in Mississippi commemorates the Civil War campaign to win the city of Vicksburg, located strategically on the ___ River.

Crack the Code

Wallace Stegner—a novelist and historian—famously wrote that national parks are "absolutely American, absolutely democratic, they reflect us at our best rather than our worst." Use the key below to crack the code and complete the famous early-twentieth-century observation by Lord James Bryce that is still quoted today.

"National Parks are the . . ."

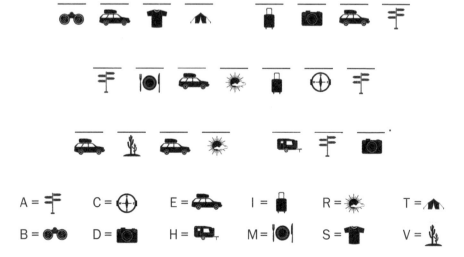

A = signpost   C = target   E = car   I = suitcase   R = sun   T = tent

B = binoculars   D = camera   H = camper   M = plate   S = shirt   V = cactus

Urban Parks

Many national parks are in urban spaces. In other words, many national parks are located in cities, places that are densely populated with people and buildings. Many of these parks are rich in history and memorialize important places, people, and events. And with the vast majority of people living in urban areas, urban parks are especially important! The Statue of Liberty National Monument in New York Harbor is a perfect example of an urban park—so is Frederick Douglass National Historic Site in Washington, D.C. The puzzle below is filled with the names of more urban parks. Use the word bank below and see if you can find the hidden words. And if you encounter a park that you've never heard of, look it up on *www.nps.gov* to learn more about it!

```
S  E  J  F  K  B  I  R  T  H  P  L  A  C  E  A  T  G
T  N  E  A  C  F  A  N  Y  N  F  A  E  G  H  L  M  O
A  A  S  T  A  O  T  O  N  A  O  D  U  N  L  I  O  L
T  T  M  A  R  R  D  F  I  M  R  O  K  N  O  N  U  D
U  I  C  A  R  T  T  E  E  L  T  N  C  Y  N  C  N  E
E  O  D  I  O  S  E  D  L  L  W  U  J  J  G  O  T  N
O  N  I  N  L  U  B  E  L  U  A  E  C  S  F  L  Z  G
F  A  M  D  L  M  N  R  B  P  S  C  T  P  E  N  B  A
L  L  E  I  T  T  Y  A  L  U  H  Q  B  A  L  M  O  T
I  M  H  R  O  E  V  L  O  M  I  D  G  T  L  E  Y  E
B  A  E  E  O  R  Q  H  V  A  N  C  A  H  O  M  H  A
E  L  L  P  L  U  E  A  E  Y  G  S  L  A  W  O  M  Q
R  L  O  H  N  T  C  L  X  O  T  U  B  R  H  R  R  C
T  I  J  D  I  U  E  L  O  F  O  R  T  P  O  I  N  T
Y  A  W  H  E  H  T  E  L  L  N  O  U  V  U  A  N  T
N  E  W  O  R  L  E  A  N  S  J  A  Z  Z  L  A  W
M  I  N  D  E  P  E  N  D  E  N  C  E  A  E  S  S  O
S  A  N  D  Y  O  U  X  I  R  O  C  K  C  R  E  E  K
```

Find the following:

STATUE OF LIBERTY   **FORT SUMTER**   **FORT POINT**
WHITE HOUSE   **FEDERAL HALL**   **GOLDEN GATE**
NATIONAL MALL   **JFK BIRTHPLACE**   **PULLMAN**
FORT WASHINGTON   **LINCOLN MEMORIAL**   **ROCK CREEK**
LONGFELLOW HOUSE   **NEW ORLEANS JAZZ**   **INDEPENDENCE**

Sudoku

PARK

	A	R	
R			A
			P
	P	K	

HIKE

H		E	
			I
I			
	K		H

ARID

A		D	
			R
R			
		I	A

NATURE

N	T			E	
R			A		
		U		T	
	T		E		
	R				A
T		A	R		

FOREST

F		R			T
S				O	
		E		R	
	R		T		
	S				O
R		O	S		

ANTLER

A	N			L	
L		E		T	N
N		L	R	E	
	E	R	N		L
E	T		L		A
	L	A		N	

TRAILS

		A	L		S
	S		T		
	T				A
A				T	
		R		S	
S			A		L

SPRING

		R	N		G
	G		S		
	S				R
R				S	
		P		G	
G			R		N

DISCOVER

D		S		I		O	V
O		V	C				R
	R				I		
I		O		C			
		D				S	
	C			O		D	I
R	S	I			E		
	D			R			S

Yosemite

ACROSS

4. The Lyell Glacier is the ___ in Yosemite and the second largest in the Sierra Nevada Mountain range.

5. In 2015 Yosemite opened the Merced ___, and for the first time kayakers were able to legally paddle the portion of the river that runs through designated parklands.

6. Half Dome is one of the most famous ___ formations at Yosemite and has a trail with steel cable handholds that leads 4,880 vertical feet from the valley floor up to the top of the dome.

8. Yosemite Falls measures 2,425 feet and is the tallest waterfall in all of North ___.

11. Yosemite is famous for its steep waterfalls, dizzying granite cliffs, and groves of giant sequoia ___.

12. The Tioga ___ runs through Yosemite and is the highest route through the Sierras in the state of California at almost 9,950 feet in elevation.

13. Much of the terrain at Yosemite was created by glaciers—large, long-lasting ice masses created by the accumulation of ___.

Historical and Cultural National Parks

ACROSS

2. The Liberty ___ is preserved at Independence National Historical Park in Philadelphia, Pennsylvania.

4. The Trail of ___ National Historic Trail commemorates the survival of the Cherokee people, who were forced by the U.S. government to leave their homelands and travel the many miles to Oklahoma on foot, horseback, and wagon.

6. Harriet Tubman repeatedly risked her life to guide almost 70 enslaved people to __; her ideals and sacrifice are honored at the Harriet Tubman Underground Railroad National Monument in Maryland.

9. The U.S.S. *Constitution* is the oldest navy warship still on the ___, and it's located in the Charlestown Navy Yard as part of the Boston National Historical Park.

11. The Wright ___ National Memorial marks the site in North Carolina where Orville and Wilbur Wright achieved the first successful airplane flights.

12. Located in New York City, the African Burial Ground National Monument is a sacred site where free and ___ Africans were laid to rest.

DOWN

1. Considered a sacred space by many Native ___, the Effigy Mounds National Monument preserves over 200 large earthen mounds located in the upper Mississippi River Valley.

3. The Women's Rights National ___ Park in New York tells the story of the first Women's Rights Convention, held in 1848.

5. The Manzanar National Historic Site in California memorializes the harrowing experiences of more than a hundred thousand Japanese Americans who were detained in military-style ___ during World War II.

7. Visitors to the Colonial National Historical Park in Virginia learn about Jamestown, the first permanent ___ settlement in America.

8. The simple beauty of the Vietnam Veterans ___ in Washington, D.C., makes a moving tribute to the men and women who served in the Vietnam War.

10. The Martin Luther King, Jr., Memorial is an urban ___ in the middle of Washington, D.C. It was completed in 2011.

Parks with Presidents

ACROSS

2. The John Fitzgerald Kennedy National Historic Site in Massachusetts preserves the president's ___ home.

4. It took four years to complete the carving of the Lincoln Statue, part of the Lincoln Memorial in ___, D.C.

7. The Washington Monument was built to honor ___ Washington.

9. Ford's Theatre in Washington, D.C., is where President ___ was assassinated in 1865.

11. Adams National Historical Park in Massachusetts honors and preserves the home of two American ___.

DOWN

1. Sagamore Hill National Historic Site in New York was known as the "Summer ___ ___" when Theodore Roosevelt was in office.

3. President's ___ in Washington, D.C., encompasses the White House, Lafayette Park, the Ellipse, and a visitor center.

5. The Franklin Delano Roosevelt Memorial in Washington, D.C., is unique in its layout, with four ___ "rooms," chronicling each of FDR's four terms in office through quotes carved in stone and bronze artwork.

6. The ___ National Expansion Memorial in St. Louis is a memorial to the role of the third president of the U.S. in opening the West.

8. In the Black Hills of South Dakota the faces of Washington, Jefferson, Theodore Roosevelt, and Lincoln were carved mostly using dynamite to create ___ Rushmore National Memorial.

10. Our first president was born on his family's ___ in Virginia. Today it is known as the George Washington Birthplace National Monument.

Junior Rangers

Kids can be rangers too! The National Park Service has a Junior Ranger program at almost all of its parks. Junior Rangers take an oath to help protect parks, to have fun learning about parks, and to share what they learn with friends and family. Kids get to explore topics like history, archaeology, geology, and astronomy. Junior Rangers receive an official certificate and patch from the National Park Service. Unscramble the words below and discover the fun things that Junior Rangers get to do.

XLEPEOR = _____

ERNAL = _____

PTORCET = _____

NSGI = _____

TIAVICITES = _____

ARSHE = _____

PALY UTOSEDI = _____

Beginnings of the National Park Service

From 1891 to 1913 the U.S. Army administrated the national parks. The earliest park rangers were soldiers—including regiments of African-American cavalry called Buffalo Soldiers—who built roads and trails and protected parks from illegal poaching and logging.

Since 1916, the National Park Service has been entrusted with the care of our national parks, safeguarding these special places and sharing their stories with millions of visitors every year. And we have visionaries like John Muir and Theodore Roosevelt to thank, both of whom are pictured here at Overhanging Rock in Yosemite National Park in 1903. Muir spent much of his life exploring Yosemite and publishing widely read articles about nature and land preservation. Muir successfully lobbied for the creation of Yosemite National Park—and his famous meeting with Roosevelt at the park led to further protections. President Roosevelt went on to champion the cause of national parks, but it wasn't until 1916 that Congress and President Woodrow Wilson created the National Park Service.

Look at the words NATIONAL PARKS. Using any combination of any number of letters found in these words, see how many smaller words you can find.

NATIONAL PARKS

NAIL	_____	_____	_____	_____
TIN	_____	_____	_____	_____
LOAN	_____	_____	_____	_____

PRESIDENT THEODORE ROOSEVELT WITH JOHN MUIR, GLACIER POINT, YOSEMITE NATIONAL PARK

Park Rules

America's national parks are great places for exploring, learning, and having fun. But in order to take care of our parks, ourselves, and each other there are some important rules that everyone has to follow. Read the "park rules" below and decide if you think they are true or false. Mark either a "T" for true or an "F" for false in the blank beside each statement.

___ 1. Feeding the animals is encouraged; especially bears because they are very hungry.

___ 2. Littering is prohibited.

___ 3. Please pick flowers and take pretty rocks home with you.

___ 4. Please pet the wild animals; they usually enjoy a good scratch behind the ear.

___ 5. Hunting is not allowed in national parks.

___ 6. No cameras are allowed in the parks.

___ 7. Campfires are allowed, but only in designated areas.

___ 8. Please don't pick up archaeological objects.

___ 9. When hiking, please stay on the designated trails.

___ 10. Tent camping is strictly forbidden in all national parks.

PUZZLE ANSWERS

America's Top Ten Most Visited National Parks

- Great Smoky Mountains
- Grand Canyon
- Yosemite
- Yellowstone
- Rocky Mountain
- Olympic
- Zion
- Grand Teton
- Acadia
- Glacier

Nature

```
H J Z C L E F R I V E R A V D P
W O R X L S E O S F J A D A I H
I F I Y I B E A R S N K M C B V
L E N K P F X A R E F P F A B P
D S X S C L A P E C S D H T K C
E S Y P A E Y C O A C T U I E A
R D B E L D B D S N A Y S O E M
N Y A U D O G W I Y J G P N A P
E C Q B P U R O P O B A D S G I
S I G H T S E E T N G D O N B N
S C T O U T S I D E S F I I O G
P C Q H A O S C P D L A T P V Z
H I K I N G T D C N T R E E S A
D M B F C P N S Y N X M K A L Y
G D A E D B E A U T Y E M A D A
E W I L D I C O S K A G I O R T
A T H S U P M S P R O T E C T P
```

Great Smoky Mountains

Grand Canyon

National Park Service

- Act
- National parks
- Acre
- Energy
- Million
- State
- Visited
- Yellowstone
- White House
- Arrowhead

Military Parks

Crack the Code

"National Parks are the best idea America ever had."

Urban Parks

```
S E J F K B I R T H P L A C E A T G
T N E A C F A N Y N F A E G H L M O
A A S T A O T O N A O D U N L I O L
T T M A R R D F I M R O K N O N U D
U I C A R T T E E L T N C Y N C N E
E O D I O S E D L L W U J J G O T N
O N I N L U B E L U A E C S F L Z G
F A M D L M N R B P S C T P E N B A
L L E I T T Y A L U H Q B A L M O T
I M H R O E V L O M I D G T L E Y E
B A E E O R Q H V A N C A H O M H A
E L L P L U E A E Y G S L A W O M Q
R L O H N T C L X O T U B R H R R C
T I J D I U E L O F O R T P O I N T
Y A W H E H T E L L N O U V U A N T
N E W O R L E A N S J A Z Z S L A W
M I N D E P E N D E N C E A E S S O
S A N D Y O U X I R O C K C R E E K
```

Sudoku

PARK

P	A	R	K
R	K	P	A
K	R	A	P
A	P	K	R

HIKE

H	I	E	K
K	E	H	I
I	H	K	E
E	K	I	H

ARID

A	R	D	I
I	D	A	R
R	A	I	D
D	I	R	A

NATURE

N	A	T	U	R	E
R	U	E	N	A	T
E	N	U	A	T	R
A	T	R	E	U	N
U	R	N	T	E	A
T	E	A	R	N	U

FOREST

F	O	R	E	S	T
S	E	T	F	O	R
T	F	E	O	R	S
O	R	S	T	E	F
E	S	F	R	T	O
R	T	O	S	F	E

ANTLER

A	N	T	E	L	R
L	R	E	A	T	N
N	A	L	R	E	T
T	E	R	N	A	L
E	T	N	L	R	A
R	L	A	T	N	E

TRAILS

T	R	A	L	I	S
I	S	L	T	A	R
R	T	I	S	L	A
A	L	S	R	T	I
L	A	R	I	S	T
S	I	T	A	R	L

SPRING

S	P	R	N	I	G
I	G	N	S	R	P
P	S	I	G	N	R
R	N	G	P	S	I
N	R	P	I	G	S
G	I	S	R	P	N

DISCOVER

D	E	S	R	I	C	O	V
O	I	V	C	S	D	E	R
C	R	E	S	D	I	V	O
I	V	O	D	C	S	R	E
V	O	D	I	E	R	S	C
S	C	R	E	O	V	D	I
R	S	I	O	V	E	C	D
E	D	C	V	R	O	I	S

Yosemite

```
        S
  C     I   W
  A     T   A
  L A R G E S T
  I       E
  F       R I V E R
  O
  R O C K
  N
  I         N
  A M E R I C A
    O       T   R
    U       I   O
    N       V   O
    T   T R E E S
R O A D     I   E
    I           V
    S N O W      E
                L
                T
```

Historical and Cultural National Parks

```
              A
              M
          B E L L
              R
              I
  H         C
  I         A
  S         N
  T E A R S     C
  O         A
  R   F R E E D O M
  I         N   P
  C   M     G   S
W A T E R   L
  L   M     I   P
      O     S   A
    B R O T H E R S
        I       K
        A
E N S L A V E D
```

Parks with Presidents

```
    W
  C H I L D H O O D
    I
    T
  P E
W A S H I N G T O N   J
  R O         U       E
  K U         T       F
    S         D       F
    E   G E O R G E    E
              O        R
              R        S
              M        O
        L I N C O L N
  F           U
  A           N
P R E S I D E N T S
  M
```

Junior Rangers

Explore
Learn
Protect
Sing
Activities
Share
Play outside

Beginnings of the NPS

Park Rules

POSSIBLE WORDS
There may be more!

Nation
Lark
Nail
Lion
Ark
Ant
Tin
Ton
Tail
Tip
In
Opal
Lap
Park
Pin
Pan
Pair
Pasta
Parka
Sin
Loan
Tan
Pal

False
True
False
False
True
False
True
True
True
False